TREATMENT:
A Collection of Poems

By

Miles Raphael

Treatment: A Collection of Poems Copyright © 2018 by Miles Raphael. All Rights Reserved.

All rights reserved. No part of this book may be reproduced in any form or by any electronic or mechanical means including information storage and retrieval systems, without permission in writing from the author. The only exception is by a reviewer, who may quote short excerpts in a review.

Cover designed by Luke Pajak

First Printing: February 2018

ISBN-13 978-1-9802850-6-9

Love and gratitude to Charles, Dan, Mira and, for eternity, Rhiannon

CONTENTS

Treatment 1
Stage I 3
Stage II 17
Stage III 29
Stage IV 55
Stage V 88

TREATMENT

I was 16. I had this thing inside me and I needed to get it out. So I wrote it down. I wrote it down again and again and again. It sat there on my laptop, it disappeared into folders and folders and more folders. Yet as the years passed I kept digging it out to add to it.

I got a new laptop, it came with it. I started a new school, it came with it. I started university, it came with it. I made new friends and it came with them. I lost old friends and it stayed in spite of them. I got my first job, it came with it. I got a new job, it came with it etc.

Nine years later and it is now apparent that it didn't come with these other things, no, I came with it. I am led by it. It - creativity, compassion, anxiety, narcissism, whatever it is - is here. It is here and it requires a proper treatment beyond the clumsy, fingerstick blood tests of private reflection.

A treatment in five stages.

Miles Raphael

Stage I - Consultation, or, Exercises in Dexterity

I will start with disinfectant and by dressing my hands in rubber gloves. It will be a consultation with much prodding, poking and flexing of the phalanges. A consultation through sight, sound, taste and touch. Practice before perfecting by reflecting on mundane and everyday occurrences.

Stage II - Preparation, or, Surgery of the Soul

Treatments can always go wrong can't they? They can always go awry? What is the harm in reaching out to greater beings than I? What harm to pray despite many questions lingering in the back of my mind? It is debatable whether these are poems or prayers, maybe they can be both?

Stage III - Operation, or, Old Fashioned Bloodletting

Surgery isn't always the best way to proceed, indeed after a consultation it is often the last resort. Yet with poetry it always seems to be the first. The chance to pry open the body and expose innards to eyes, nose and air is too great to resist. Once the door to the heart is open, it's all too easy to push pins into the flaps of skin formerly belonging to the chest to keep it open. These poems are possessed by love, hate and it's vague and indistinct offspring.

Stage IV - Rehabilitation, or, Talking Doctors

The body has had enough attention, the mind also needs to be addressed so that It can come to terms with the trauma of surgery. So that It can understand how best to live with its new body and make suitable plans for the future. Poems pledged to common sense.

Stage V - Ongoing Medication, or, Drugs

Yet for as much as I have done there will always be more to do afterwards. It has been treated but It will need to be treated time and time again. Provisions for this will need to be made, residual waste will need to be siphoned and expelled. Once you've started, it can be hard to know when to stop...

TREATMENT

STAGE I

Consultation, or, Exercises in Dexterity

Where I partake in poetic exercises to stretch the mind and ready the fingers, to provide a lyrical varnish to otherwise inconsequential or imagined happenings.

Box

Box: black, squashed ends
Folded and crumpled
Almost looking sad
had it expressions to show
or heart to beat
or lungs to exhale.
But it is just a box
Empty of contents
Spinning in place
Soon to disintegrate.

TREATMENT

Villa

Nothing quite like it;
the slap of bare feet
on newly warmed stone
during holiday retreat.

Early in the morning
Yet not with lack of sleep
Softly, on back beneath the awning
Cold eyes, warm feet.

Ducks

When walking, trainers cup the cracks
Fixing temporarily what has snapped
The concrete split like so many seams in crumpled paper
Litter like autumnal leaves
Rain stained brickwork, acid leaves its kiss
Across the bridge, a swamp sits beneath
Yet somehow, miraculously, ducks can be seen
Unbothered that what should be blue is green
They live; it's as simple as it seems.

TREATMENT

Sweat

It hasn't rained in weeks
Your sweat is a lie
As it drips in fat drops
Through pinhole pores
To grow double in size
Hanging off an eyelash
Flashes of blindness
You taste the sweat through
your forehead
It's wetter than your dry tongue
And softer than your caked, cracked lips.

Waking Up

Feet out from beneath the bedding
Cool outside its cotton white
The dark underneath covered in cream
And the toes stretch and twist,
becoming self-aware
Talking to itself as though of own mind
And on your back as you twiddle your toes
You lie covered in milk and cream
Before the day beckons.

TREATMENT

Semblance

The written word is deceptive
When treated as an analogue to speech
It acts more as paint on paper
than sounds uttered through parted teeth.

The alphabet is to page
as drops of rain on a window pane.

"Meaning" curves to understanding
as colours blend to reveal a still life,
an abstract statement, or some other sort
of treated scene.

Snowflake

Like spiderwebs
They cover the concrete
Sickly spirals, white in colour
Capable of catching others
It's a cold day and Winter hovers
Set to offer gelid wonders
Enticing children
[or car crash cries:]
"causing horror."

TREATMENT

Hearse

Carried inside the hearse
Was little more than air
It was not a day for the dead
So its innards lay bare
How closely an undertaker's hearse
Resembles a magician's box!
One might wonder if insanity or desperate hope
Ever inspired one of the drivers to load the back with bodies
Chop it into sectors
Spin the car in a circle and knock three times
To see if the dead might rise.

Drunk

"It's like walking on water"
Is all I can think
Stumbling through this night-time London street.
Cars come at me like waves
Other people; crabs, marlins, cod beneath my feet.

My head is not with my legs
My legs without my neck
As though my spinal cord has been snapped, plucked, pulled
Much like a spine peeled from a prawn a tourists eats
as I drunkenly knock the sandwich away from her teeth.

I am the alcohol I have consumed
All lights blurry, blinding, confusing
The crowd parts as no one else wants to be near me
The crowd parts as though falling beneath me
"It's like walking on water"
Now my body water is more cocktail than chemical

I'll have a double hydrogen and oxygen for the road.

TREATMENT

Adjective: Alienated

Like a hole in a pocket
Of well-worn jeans
Too comforting to toss out
But too large to fill with things
So these jeans are worn daily,
then weekly, then only
in the privacy of home
Where pockets are not needed
So nothing can fall out.

Adjective: Hate

Like sickle cell
Like sick little cell
Shaped to cut
A perfect shape
But a poor fit
An error, a mistake
To carry oxygen
From place to place
Cutting its own vessels
Choking with distaste.

Hatred is a sickle cell
Misshapen for its purpose
But still of perfect shape.

TREATMENT

Adjective: Gluttonous

A dog's memory is short
It will lick the hand that feeds and keep eating until it is full.
Cover its eyes, lay down more food and continue to eat,
it will.
Much to its own harm, survival is not instinctive at all.
The more ragged the dog, the more primal and starved,
The more it will gorge despite its slack water-bottle belly;
distended, enlarged.
You can see meat undissolved, poking through the flesh; two layers of ribs.
Eating till eating hurts.
Till pain has a taste, burped food and vomit on teeth.

Daydreaming

Groping in times tired
For something to hold dear
As age becomes days
and living becomes years
Pulled through the broken silence
To land with yawns and puckered eyes
Trapped in incoherence
When tying dreams to waking
life.

TREATMENT

STAGE II

Preparation, or, Surgery of the Soul

Where I enter a communion with God, faith, faithlessness and the eternal.

Face

"I am wearing my face,"
The sun spares the window from shade
and obliterates my reflection
As it falls and reforms upon
my eyes, nose, lips and cheeks.
If I close my eyes
I can see the gap between
fat, flesh, teeth and skin
And feel the strings
As sunlight clings
And holds my face to my being.

TREATMENT

Greater

So thirsty you imagine blood to flow
Between the fold page that is your flat lips
Dry weight not wet
It wouldn't tip the scale
Nevertheless
You do not sip as the enemy offers
water; pure, mountain tears
Your eyes copy mountain
As they flow with saltwater your lips would
love to drink.
Yet
You do not drink
Lips relax the grimace; spasmolytic.
Were your spirit to be weighed
Its mass could not be read
So strong, so sanctified, so majestic.
You are so much greater than this!

In All

Do you remember all the silent sobs,
cries without tears, sound or spit?
Times where you have delivered and I
have, in my ignorance, ignored it?
Days when all has gone to plan and
with a knowing eye, I raise palms to the sky.
Nights when in a drunken stupor drastic acts
seem reasonable and without spite.
With knee bent on soft cushion of church pews
Or knee damp from stopping in a puddle to tie
rebellious shoes.
In all you are present: in darkness, ignorance
knowledge, love and truth.

TREATMENT

Faithless, or, The Sinner's Lamentation

Oh God what have I done?
Or rather failed to do...
With so much time spent empty of you
My decay is gradual, it's growth natural
I am becoming the nothing that I do
Oh God what have I done?
Or rather failed to do...
Why oh why am I again without?
Why does emptiness consume so much?
Why is "why" all I can urge myself to mutter?
Questions asked without expectation of an answer.

Star

I can see stars.
Despite the cities struggle against their shine,
They are bright.
So my naked eyes roll in a nervous fidget,
Afraid to blink and miss a second of their existence
But with the wonder comes a ridiculous longing
A nauseating spasm of the mind and a wicked teasing of the heart
I want to be a star, a piece of the black beyond this ball.
I want to be the meaning, I want to see it all.

TREATMENT

15 Questions

1. Will it be the same as yours?
2. Will it last for years, months or be shorter?
3. Is it going to hurt?
4. Will I cry from pain or scream from fear?

Due to distance I doubt you can hear this or remember your tears...

5. Do you remember anything that happened before?
6. Or, once it happens, does that door forever close?
7. Once it's over will I have the answers to these questions or will nothing of me remain to receive benediction?
8. Is it going to hurt?
9. Please, I need to know, will it be worse than the kind of pain experienced on this earth?
10. Or is it bliss?
11. Is the euphoria everlasting or simply lasting as long as the passing takes?
12. Are you still caught in that moment when the seal to that other place breaks?
13. Like waves upon a beach, does it rise and fall to ultimately never cease?
14. Can you, where you are, speak, smile, wince or smirk?
15. Is it where this all ends or a new start?

It is Finished

Attempting to close my burning hand
I cannot, stuck as it is and pierced by iron
But Lord how I want to!
I am the Lord and I say you cannot
But what son can be said to be loved,
when that son dies nailed to a cross?
Is it right of me to die and correct to leave the earth
When in this exquisite pain, I regret my very birth!

It's a burning, burning heat
The shaft inside my hand
My fragmented mind is Helios, Ra, Sol,
Sun, no longer son of Man.
No longer of single mind,
No longer phrased through an "I"
Burning hand speaks of own accord
As living God dies but to be reborn.

TREATMENT

Agape

What is love to a God?
Is it easy or hard to adore and admonish
To care for and cherish
Millions upon millions of small simple beings
Who can't even agree what you are!
Or who you are?
Or even if you are?
Do you exist?
Ask and you will find as many replies
as eyes attached to embodied minds
Who can say "are you mine?"
Yet each reply is but a lie for certainty they cannot find.

I wonder, is love as elusive as a God
that so many lean on in trialing times
Yet cannot count among the many others
they would consider, friend, kin and kind?

A Religious Experience

I saw the spire rise
A steeple amongst the trees
Looking fake and manmade
as though a Hollywood backdrop
Flat and pressed thin against the sky,
telling eyes nothing of the God inside
But still I saw it rise
And rain fell as though its tip had burst the sky
And tears fell as though the rain poured through my mind
"This is real," whispered a voice inside
Before my bus arrived.

TREATMENT

Father

In strong, open arms
No need to be afraid
The hair of manhood locks
with your prepubescent locks
Forearms thick like tree trunks
Your spindly limbs more like twigs
encouraging you to rest upon the bark
So rest upon the bark
Sleep.

Introspection

At times I want to drop
And fall onto the ocean of my dreams
Floating in exhaustion
Floating, weightless, slight
Gently hanging in existence
Only loosely tied to life
Dropping into the all-consuming sea
Anchorless and cast adrift
In the waters of my being.

TREATMENT

STAGE III

Operation, or, Old Fashioned Bloodletting

Where I share melancholic aphorisms and explore sentimental matters.

30 July 2008

Sometimes when I open my mouth,
The words just seem to tumble out
Drip drop in the swash and flow
Falling more purposelessly
Causing only more drops to fall,
And soon I am drenched, soon I am drowning
as if I never learned how to swim
Yet somehow I float!
Coincidence or not,
Dead bodies
tend to
float.

Childish Lovers

Punch me, pinch me, kick me
Does it mean that we're in love?
When we were children, nervous stomach
would cause twitches in my arms
I'd push you into puddles and catch you afterwards
because no one knows love like a child.

So punch me, pinch me, kick me
So I know that we are in love
Don't stare silently at the TV
and end every message with a full stop.
Don't tell me that we need to talk
Yet when we do it's about what do we want for dinner, who is doing the washing?
Whose turn is it to pay for the weekly shopping?
Who is doing the bare minimum to maintain this façade?
How are we so childish without being childishly in love?

Little Mores

Do a little more, just a little more, always a little more
To regret that little more, to repent for that little more
To want for no more because all those "little mores" cause
little shames, little pains and little sores.

Until all the "little mores" are so many that they,
like a broken sieve,
cannot contain the feelings they were supposed to
sift from the negative and unnecessary.
Blotting out all the good
Until sunrise is as sunset.

TREATMENT

Pilgrim God

Grimace, self-hate, repeat
Complain, complain, condemn
Apologise then repeat
Always repeat
For in this cycle you are both
Pilgrim and God
And as God you choose
To hate the sin not the sinner
Hate the sin not the sinner
And you grimace
Not because you hate what you
Do
But because
Your discontent says that you are not the sin
Your discontent shows a pity and a disdain for circumstances
As though it's a shame that things cannot be different
What more can one expect from one who self-supplicates?

A Pilgrim God
Who walks on coals
Pretending to feel aching and hurt.

Pilgrim
You want the God inside you
To know
That he should hate the sin
Hate the sin
Grimace
Repeat.

Narcissism

"Who else imagines themselves as beautiful?
Hands up please
No, do not stand on tiptoes
Lest, the others, I cannot see!"
Hands shoot up in pairs then threes
But I cannot count the total
Lost as I am in my own raising arm
The slip of the sleeve
The bowed back, cocked chest and the
tender smirk on moist lips.

TREATMENT

Ugly

Some days I want to be ugly and showered in alms,
Because arms are too afraid to touch my nouveau rubella.
Stuck inside layers of scab and skin
Coated in the stuff so thick
No one would think
To expect anything of the organism within.

Some days I want to be ugly
In a quiet and inoffensive way
Bland and pathetic like a garden slug
Surrounded by salt before inhalation and rust.
Ugly in a way that satisfies the ache
Without attracting the gaze, pity or disdain
Of other living things
Whether they are close or faraway.

Some days I want to be ugly
In an objective sort of way,
Not attached to an insult or meant to injure
Ugly in a way that calls forth:
Passive and correct.
Satisfying the rotten breath
of an unhappy, dulled and exhausted soul.

Some days I want to be ugly in a way that makes sense.
In a way that is simple and un-complex.

Watchman

Wrapped in a blanket of my own ideas,
Is where I feel most at home.
I listen to my voice as it bounces around the empty rooms
and across the vacant floors made of neurons and sinew.
But it's very sad, isn't it?
It's so lonely when your world is held captivate
and becomes a panopticon of which you are the sole
watchman.

TREATMENT

The Leech

You never showed a voice for it!
No desire to sing and croon
Than why do you chirp
at the earliest reminder
of the very thing
that what you never
wanted to do?
When you find it to bring happiness to those closest to you.

Entropy, or, We Tend to the End

Planting flowers that will someday die
Raising young who will leave us behind
Starting jobs that will require we retire
Cooking meals that must be eaten or else expire
Reading books as we cup the final page
Introducing ourselves to strangers with aplomb
even though few of these friendships will last for very long
And rising each morning to find ourselves back in bed.
Sleeping is to dreams as living is to death.

TREATMENT

Hypocrite

Inside a desperate irritation
That prevents you from relaxing
And sits atop your head, fondling your ears
drunk and with hairy fingers

The feeling, I mean, so gross and fat as to be bodied
It's fucking irritating
Your own hypocrisy, lowering your standards
because on a superficial level it sounds good; it's catchy.

"Yeah it sounds good alright?"
You both argue and ask as that ape of a
feeling grinds against you.

Now that You Mention It

Now that you mention it
I realise that I cannot be in love
The good I did was not good enough
Or perhaps too good
Or more than we deserved
Because the things I did for you
Placed me beyond the heart
Placed me beyond the tongue
We can talk about what happened
You can thank me all you like
But my bruised hands and knees
Tell us both any lust would be a lie
I have seen you undressed
Not of clothes but of skin
And when you reached your lowest
It was just you, the devil and me
So how can I propose
How can I move from hands and knees to knee?
When now that you mention it
I've done too much for us to be.

Paranoia

His preference was to people watch
because of fears inside of his head:
"It is better to watch people than to be
watched by them instead."

Shadow

A shadow is a sign of an obstacle,
and it is made by the blocking of light
Often presenting a warped shape
tall and gaunt or widened at the hips.
A shadow is light blocked by object.

So the word seems apt to describe
certain lives lived such; left tall and gaunt
or widened at the hips.
Like a doodle on lined paper, crumpled
when unfolded leaving a deformed impression
of what was originally a work of art.

Certain lives left opaque and malformed
by a thick lump, blocking its light source.

TREATMENT

Ugly Duckling

A mother tells her son stories of an ugly duckling every night
for his first five years until with comfort he takes the book
and until with confidence he reads it himself.

And a son reads and reads until the ugly duckling grows into
a swan and a little story in an anthology grows into bigger
books and a son reads enamoured with the tale. Ready to
believe he will similarly fill out
pure
pretty and swelled.

But a son now of age to have sons and raise them right,
comes to learn that his mother lied.
Not due to malicious intent but to encouraging such stories
as he laid down and fell asleep in his bed.

He now sought to correct what he saw as the greatest
misstep and with pen, paper and glue he tore out the last
page and replaced it with something he felt was true:

*"Alone in his pond the ugly duckling cannot know beauty
even as a swan
With many other birds each vying for a drop of water they
can call their own.
And in the mad rush with little space to spread his wings
He has no one to acknowledge either his ugliness or his beauty
And lost as he is, gone is his inherent swan's gift.
Mimicking above sea-level the chaos of his feet."*

You're a Bright Kid

1. Xxxxx + Xxxxx - Xxxxx = Xx? Xxxxx. (1 mark)
a. You state the fucking obvious after studying our lives like I cannot study my life like I cannot study at all because your teachers refused to teach like your teachers refused me entry.

2. Xxxx xxxx (xxxxxxxxx)? (1 mark)
a. Sure I have a seat in the classroom and a record on a computer but it's all a box to tick, I'm just a box so tick. Go on.

3. Xxx xxxxxxx xxxxxx xxxxx xxxxxxxxxxxxx xxxxx? Xxxx? (2 marks)
a. The cane may be replaced by arguments, interactive whiteboards and class trips to Coventry but you beat me all the same.

4. Xxxxx xxx xxxxxx (xxxx+xxxx)(xxxx-xxxx)? (4 marks)
a. Neglect is abuse in all but name.

5. Xxx xxx xxxx? XxxxxxxXXX (4 marks)
a. I'm boring, I'm poor, disruptive, yes you're bored. Keep me in a hole and applaud my ascent as though inspiring, as though a lesson of what you can accomplish if you imbibe the cane.

6. Xxxx xxxx xx x (xxxxxxx%)? (5 marks)
a. Study me, study me, study me. Do what you must do to earn your wage, do what you must to explain away this disgrace.

TREATMENT

Reasons

There is a reason why statues decay
With little more than wind and rain
Drops of wet can crack a mountain
Lines in wood, collapse a house
Day in day out the tiny troubles
Can buckle and coerce a shout
Yes there is a reason why Pisa stumbles
Like elephant afraid of little mouse.

Whine

"It's a bitter wine"
Boy we've heard it time
and time again
Your breath stinks
Your skin is yellowed, are you sick?
"It's a bitter wine," whine, whine, whine
Your yellow belly, jaundiced skin
Coward's flight from reality.

TREATMENT

Bedfellows, or, My Fears for Sacco, Vanzetti and Others Since

There is honour in your death
In your written receipt of innocence
Published, your letters have poetic elegance
Greatness is your bedfellow
Said poetic...

The poetic is said, observed
Not seen, lived, or experienced from within.
You cannot return with your receipt or
exchange your lot for another
So, seen from within, your
bedfellow is the cool side of the blanket,
the wooden box or the tin pot.

About You

I've spent all night thinking about you
You're projected onto the inside of my eyelids
So sleep only enters me into a vision
Rather than closing me from the visible,
made manifest is the invisible!
That being my burgeoning affection for you.

I see you more clearly than my fingers and thumb held
at arm's length in my pitch-black bedroom.
I feel you more keenly than the covers draped around my
hips
Thanks to the heaviness of my chest
My laboured breaths, open lips and now
suddenly
uncomfortably
warm
Feel as though I should undress
But body pressed to blanket, cold and oppressive,
Is the realisation that this 75% cotton is not your skin.

Get out of my head and into my bed, hand on phone wants
to say
Yet I do not want to scare you away
As I do not want you to think sex is what dictates my fervour
Though of course it plays a role
I want to wrap and roll my arms around you
Feel your breath on my neck, your lips on my chest
As you talk directly to my heart and say "yes, yes, yes"
To every single question I have not asked yet.

I am still thinking about you and writing this has not helped.
I can only feel cotton and my heavy breaths are without an echo.

TREATMENT

Emotions

You're left feeling it...
That slow, cold and lonely;
that fog of unknowing.

In joy, pain, love and loathing
Unable to contain or explain
this galloping beast of emotion.

It spreads covering in a
thick solvent.
"Don't inhale, open window...circulation"
Is what you would read on the label
Could you bottle and contain
This thing; vague and unnamed.

Children of the Overdraft

There is a woman who on her way to work
Has a realization that is cause for concern
Her monthly wage cannot agree
With the money pouring out annually
With little qualifications and no contacts of this earth
She visits the cemetery to seek counsel
from those life spurned
It is to no avail for the dead do not speak
in a language that is financially enlightening.

TREATMENT

I Work Harder than You & Deserve my Wealth

Sun stained skin: a jaundiced yellow
with puffy fat stomach like a sick babe.
On a thousand beads of gold into which
feet sink and leave stains.
A blood baron money rich and thick with sin
Enjoys his millions.

Oh Night

Oh long, long night
Do not echo the clock
I know you are silent
because it is time to sleep
I know you embrace your children
like eyelids closed tight over pupils
like pupils fast asleep in class
Urged to rest by the gentle hum
and vibration of their teacher's voice.

Oh long, long night
In your silence do not echo
The stark, hard tick of time.
Give me another five minutes
Give me another five hours
Give me another five years
Hide me from the dawn and protect me from a day
That approaches with such menace it keeps me awake.

TREATMENT

Writer's Guilt

I touch my fevered forehead
With my zealous pen
It's a cold evening isn't it?
Alone in single bed
Trying to galvanise, when
I should rest...

Empty pages, soft fingers and unblemished tips
Guilt overwhelms
Work harder
Earn sleep.

Fear and Insecurity

Surely this is a sickness of an unforgivable nature?
Pages and pages, gigabytes of literature
All consumed with "I"

Without substantial growth of ability
Lacking confidence and basic rhythm
You're not a poet or a lyricist
Stop pretending that you are.

STAGE IV

Rehabilitation, or, Talking Doctors

Where I try to reappraise destructive thoughts, feelings, images and tendencies to offer them their proper place.

Miles Raphael

Love and Insecurity

I am a child who has stumbled after learning to walk
Afraid that my feet are not well taught
That they have lied to me when they promised to move forward
Yet here I sit on my arse with tears forming
But oh how I want to walk!
Oh how I want to go outside!
So despite my insecurity I will stand and stride
In this way, I anxiously continue to write
So large is the pit in my belly for words, rich and ripe!
I will continue with this endeavour
As a growing child switches between laughing and crying
When faced with testing times.

TREATMENT

Influence

When I pause to look at my influences
They make a mosaic of me
Cracked glass and uneven lines of glue
The words of those around me,
The state of my community and my family
All that I grow through
Sometimes you must step back to see the full view.

I will tell you about a time when
I was influenced in a manner most divine
I don't remember my age but can still feel the look on my face
History is found in memory and not stacks of facts
It's our subjective feelings that hold truth
Not age, not a mathematical proof
But I digress – I am talking about the first pages of a book
From the beginning of *Notes from the Underground* I was hooked
The pull of my eyes, twitch of my lips
As though a child smiling at the wind
My visage was twisted into a half smirk/ half bewildered kiss
Locked forever with the memory of it.

I have continued writing with the belief that "I can"
Thanks to Fyodor a long since decomposed corpse
directs the actions of this living, breathing man.

Despite this I did resist,
I hated being easily led
Feeling influenced left me feeling dread
That I might not be "me" but might be instead
A pastiche of those I call friend, enemy, mum and dad.
Yet at times it can be the opposite and fill me with

encouragement
To be a continuation rather than a singular, solitary thing
Knowing that "me" is as much a part of the world as the sun and the air
The bugs, bees and law of gravity
It has gravity.
I into him, he into me, her into us, us into we.

I feel weight as I speak, the weight of lumps in my throat billows my cheeks
Knowing that influence is dirt cheap
It's not only for the great or the powerful, not just the mighty and tall
Sometimes it can be found in a friendly stranger, a cold fist or
the lessons learned from a hungry mouth.
Aspects of our encounters take hold
They become totems, myths and encoded in our souls.

Influence is such a potent word for such a common thing
I can share more experiences of how frequently it's seen
Follow me a short way back to 2016
A supply teacher is what I had been
Where they dropped me in to teach who was left
Once teacher called in sick and couldn't reach their desk.
Inexperienced and untrained, I just did what I was told
I am nobody special, I have not a name that you should know
Yet even in my quiet role my influence was on show
Pupil after pupil as they came to know my face
Asked me about friendship, religion, their futures, their fate
Before the dawn of their exams or ahead of a family break
I influenced the actions of those around me
Just through trying to relate.

I in turn learned from them and from others I have met

TREATMENT

Without intending to learn a lesson, I am a student time and
time again
Feeling in my tongue new phrases and inflections,
thoughts, ideas and dreams
Chasing new perspectives to find the joy in being me.

I started on a lie and for this I must apologise
Influencing and influenced – a mosaic of discourse
I encouraged the use of binoculars:
"Step back to see your universe"
Yet I've spent this whole time stepping in
and stepping through
Because who am I to separate?
What you do for me and I in turn do for you.

Potential Father

Through the eyes of the son
When son is aged (potential father)
Sees potential unfulfilled
For the father (though he doesn't know his son)
Is the father whom son still grew from.

As the eyes see upside down,
Leaving an image to be corrected by the mind
So too does the son see himself out of line
Until realisation acts as brain with eye
To realign the son with the father
So that son might realise that these faults belong to the father
They are kin not kind.

See through the eyes of the father
So you might not be blind
To the faults, fears and frets
Belonging to childhood,
yet steering your adult life.

TREATMENT

"Better Back Then"

"It was always better back then,"
and the loss is of an antiseptic sort
Rubbing, scouring, cleans the prints
and pocks of past:
"It was better back then
and safer back then
and we were smarter back then
and we were bolder back then…"

This wanderlust and longing;
this fetish for the past
Is born of temporal brains
aware that they and their bodies
deconstruct and decompose
and break apart and are fed to worms and other bugs.

A sterile hurt, a sterile package
Born of bleached thoughts
Stained beige by faded memories,
and an awareness of the ports of death and birth.

'Cuffs

Wrists so slender they
cannot bear the girth of 'cuffs
and wilt as though rickets strewn
with any weight no matter how small or large.

Strange enough the tiny hands will try to reattach
the plastic armlets as they slip off time and time again.
"They do not fit," says a voice not in bodies head
Until it eventually tires of yelling empty words
at dishonest and unhearing hands.

This body is not alone as others attempt to copy
Each one picking up 'cuffs strewn along the aisle
Perusing then picking one's that from afar appear to fit
To merrily leave the jail with the regular clang of dropping
metal.

So many slender wrists pick up 'cuffs that cannot fit
To pardon oneself from crimes one did not commit
So strange is the sight of many a galled intelligentsia
Arguing against their conviction, when they alone have
concocted the sentence.

TREATMENT

Instances

Needless to say,
more often than not,
These instances of wrong represented
no culture whatsoever.

They were just flecks of scabbed
and raised skin.
Instances.
Rightfully abhorred.
Nothing more.
And never rightfully extended
to encompass more.

Miles Raphael

The Stations of Your Cross

It's 16:34, what excuse do you have?
"I'm just lacking, lacking"
It's easy to say, feeling soggy, sagging
Feeling heavy as though your body is your cross
Then lift your body, lift your cross
Walk your Calgary, march along
"But I'm lacking, lacking
lacking, lacking, lacking."

It's 16:35, a minute has passed but it's
only a minute and for all you "lack"
You'll have many minutes more
You may be thinking you're lacking but time
is your Simon of Cyrene, now come on, rise.

TREATMENT

Come to Me as a Human

No one asks the question
No one cries to know
"Why do you live?"
"What do you live for?"
It's always other issues,
Always other concerns
There are always more important things that
"We" need to know.
But no one ever questions and explains
Why should I care?
Why should anyone care?
That you were born.

What good is this question?
What cry for attention?
As if you had chosen to exist on this earth
But you did choose to write
You did choose to sing
To philosophise, lead nations and
make machines
To share these self-centred things
And so I think it's fair to ask
And quite sensible to know
Not your nugget of wisdom,
That will change my world
But the 'you' that is being implicitly hoisted
Into my personal concerns
Do share
Why anyone should care
Why you yourself
Need to socialise
Forget the importance
Forget the changes or the weight

Come to me as a human
Or else I'll care not about the world
your hobbies shape.

TREATMENT

Vanity

I know what you think you are
Yellowed milk soured in the sun
Starting to curdle, so curdled it
crumbles to touch.

Yes I know what you think you are
A self-absorbed Neanderthal
caught up in corrupt afterthoughts
of last afternoons unimportant regrets.
I know what you think you are.

Yes I know that the things you think could fill
buckets too heavy to hold one handed and yet
still you'd try.
Thoughtlessly lifting with the right
as the left cleans your brow in sullen disbelief.

Miles Raphael

Swords in Civil Times

Why open curtains when you can
cut the cloth with your sword?
Perched beside your lap in your repose
Hands on knees, priestly and sweetly
Warriors are not ones to stall.

So cut the curtains, cut them true,
Cut them down so that the sun can shine through
And cut the door, hack it away with your blade
So that you might begin your day
And cut the laces on your shoes,
When you find that your bladed hand
lacks the dexterity to untie the laces so that they
might be removed from you.

Just be wary that when your shirt starts to smell
You cut with care lest you lop off something else
Something more precious than your outfit…
Out-fit, or rather ill-fit, you don't fit it seems to me
Yet still in hand; sword will not leave you be.

TREATMENT

The Salesman's Creep

Ten ticks on the wall is not enough
to reassure, the salesman who needs
ten more and again after that another score.

Bitten fingernails spill pink and throbbing red
So bright it covers the yellow caused by nervous puffs on
cigarette
So bright because constant pressure caused by pen allows no
time for rest
Until the day that fingers stiffen from early RSI; onset.

Who has time to count or time to measure,
the time spent inking cursive scabs into the ledger?
But time is spent, time and time again
On checking with anxiety that the ticks are never
lonely, on the contrary they must spread!
But lonely is the man or woman who finds
themselves with dread
Checking daily with quivering pen
If they have done enough to pay the rent
If they have done enough to creep ahead.

There is a collection of books collecting dust on many
shelves
and many more websites getting clicks but little else.
Indeed for every eye that falls upon such pages
Another two have tried to join these multitudinous "sages"
But what sort of books have been described?
What is this panacea that has been thusly digitised?
The texts taken to task are the many businessman's guides,
the self-help "go-getter" genre that seeks to empower and
aggrandise
It remains to be seen how many of these buyers

have consequently been brought to wealth
Or if any shame is felt by such writers who offer snake oil
to the very snakes themselves.

And of this sorry state, I as one with time to spare
Find myself ticking on my own record with despair
The number of ways in which a salesman must behave untoward
And act in ways most concerning and morally bankrupt
The salesman's creep, is a crawl towards thievery,
callousness and all else that is corrupt.

TREATMENT

Dust

My eyes roll up to see
Dust draped upon the lampshade
Grey hangs over bright:
Like the sun beneath cloudy sky
Resembling silvered ivy as the residue
slinks around the chord
It's a strange sight to see
such a light
Shining despite its burden;
despite its blight.

Hands/ Heart

Hands so big
It's a wonder your heart fits
inside your body at all.
Isn't it true that your heart
shares size with a balled fist?
Isn't it also true that a heart
can either be open or closed?
Like a hand or a fist.

TREATMENT

Love

A bit of love
A better love
Or a bitter love?
A bit of love
A better love
Or a bitter love?

Which one is it? Which one of the three best explains
The kind of love one must have for their mistakes?
This question could consume any kind of misstep
but I am thinking of one that is especially permanent
Like what happens when you find yourself with a child
So hard to love the colour drains from the feeling
To leave an outline, empty, cold and self-deceiving?

I am not a father though I know many others
And as my friends form families of their own I have been
forced to reassess the one from which I have grown
Now, my father receives no love from me
He's less than five miles away yet is someone I never want
to see
I feel his unease on the few occasions where we clash
Sometimes, I guess, I wonder what it must be like to have a
child you can't understand.

Let me get off of that path as he doesn't deserve the empathy
or the time
But the wider question is not so easily released from my
mind.
Yes let's imagine this shame I feel for my father
Was instead felt for a son or a daughter
There are enough decent people with sadistic sons and
dolorous daughters

Who had no hand in causing them trauma
Yet cannot find a way to stop them from hurting themselves
and others.
So what is it to be? What is most correct?
A bit of love for those hate claimed?
A better love than they deserve?
Or a bitter love because fuck it you made them and they are
yours
So how can you choose not to love what love spawned?

I would like to take a closer look
At each type of love I might find myself feeling
Were I condemned to adore
A child capable of the most depraved acts of violence, cruelty
and torture.

A bit of love might be the best dish
To serve to selfish, callous lips
Occupy the middle ground between affection and mistrust.
Accept that your neighbours will gossip about failures of
your parenthood.
Admit that mistakes were made
                            though you don't know what they were
That prison might be the best place
                            and you fear the day they get out
Continue to visit them once a week
Trying to save the silence from the sentiments your
damaged goods will leak
As malice and contempt is dispensed whenever they speak.

Yet whenever you meet
You see yourself and your partner
Inside this nephilim
And for a moment they escape their shackles
By reminding that once upon a time you held within your

TREATMENT

arms
A cherubim.

Maybe this reminder is so intoxicating
Instead of just a "bit of love" you are overflowing with the stuff.
You adore them with a "better love," one that is bolder, bulging, bent…
While admirable in its own right, left with this commitment
Your own hands will be soiled
As you must condone and excuse, participate and become enthused
With your child's tragic pursuits.
Your morals will be drowned in your love
Your hobbies and habits, waterlogged, dizzy as though drunk
Friends and family will be cast overboard
It's just you and your child beyond good and evil.

What a quixotic commitment to make!
So extreme as to seem perverse, or at least, quite strange
That being the case, perhaps there is another way?

You could offer your child a bitter love
One that stings if dry lips take a sip
Cracks in your relationship are cleansed of filth
Leaving cracks clean yet uncomfortably visible.
Yes, your love is laced with honesty and grit.
You don't ignore their lack of empathy
In fact you try to atone for it!
You try to understand with a surgical mistrust
The patterns in their behaviour that cause nothing but harm.
You accept this burden and your share of the blame
You apologise for the things they have done time and time again.

Without denying that you've lived two distinct lives to date
One before your child and another after their seed escaped.

So I hope you see why I repeat with dismay
A bit of love
A better love
Or a bitter love?
A bit of love
A better love
Or a bitter love?

I don't know how you should behave
However as long as love is involved
Your child will have a home and a connection to the tree
from which they came.
And as a parent – from prehistory to the present day
That's the most essential act of care you can provide
To give them a chance to find some sort of peace
Inside of their hearts, souls and minds.

TREATMENT

Body Language

The body doesn't lie;
lying is an ability possessed only by the mind.
Vocal chords, alone, can employ such a skill to distract and mislead
But the tongue, fingers, eyes and lips
Do not know how to use such tricks.

So as your mind races against the elapsing time
Between my last utterance and your turn to speak
Whatever you say to make this easier for yourself
Is not the truth, no, it is a trick.

These excuses are cute.
They are not strong, not convincing and not resolute.
You can say that you are unsure, that you don't know what to do
That this has a simple solution, namely, that I should forget about you
But your fingers linger just a second too long
Yes, you return the touch as my hands run along your arm
Every opportunity that there is to be close
You reciprocate with weight, warmth and longing.
Your hesitation is premeditated
Yet I have no confidence that a crime is forthcoming.

So please take as much time as you need
To perform this mental accountancy
I'll wait until you learn that the body doesn't lie
And it has already decided my affection is perfect, pure and fine.

Miles Raphael

A Wider Acceptance

For the love of strangers
Is how we spend our days
In constant appeasement of
the "Other" inside of our brains
Picking the right shoes, and
expressions on the train
How few and sweet the days,
When not on the chase.

TREATMENT

Please Hold the Rail

He couldn't stop from falling on the train
Legs firm but flimsy hands flailed at formless air
It was a rough landing
The thud caused others to stare at this foolhardy gentleman
Who believed hands in pockets and a thoughtful gaze
Were ample protection against sudden turns, breaks and sways.
He quickly arose and rejected hands to help
Straightening his shirt until he again looked ready to present,
An outfit he had prepared for strangers who did not care.

The fall, it seemed, did little to remind
That one shouldn't be preoccupied with superficial designs.

Jealousy

Jealousy is the knife that cuts the cake
A necessary tool to take a piece
But how big to make the pieces and to whom are they dispersed?
Is it right to cut a single piece or better to cut many for all?

Jealousy is needed to take a piece from twelve
But if unrestricted it leaves not a piece for anyone else!
And renders sick the one who cuts
To serve as a reminder to trust your gut
Over eyes that are prone to lust.

TREATMENT

Christmas Grin

At certain times of the year
One is expected to be merry
Faking a smile and trading
humility for humility
Sitting round a tree
Adorned in drunk authority
One is expected to be merry
and empty of misery.

And yet I've heard a fake smile
Is a splitting of the cheeks still
And a grin no matter its plasticity
Can assuage a suspicious will
Yes even an unhappy Christmas
Can offer pockets of mirth
If you sink into its simplicity
And allow a smile to spread,
massage the cheeks,
console the heart
and consort the head.

Miles Raphael

Alive

You're alive, aren't you?
Yet you're looking for your life
As though you dropped it along the way
and need to retrace your steps.
But you can't return or pick up like a penny
that which you bear at every minute.
Remember your life is you
And not out there waiting,
Not stuck to gum on the pavement
Let others do whatever they will
You have no obligation to be anyone else but you!

TREATMENT

Celebrate

Growing up I was often left to myself
I had little in the way of encouragement
So I leaned on stories to learn truths and guard my mental health
But they could only teach so much
And at their worst they made me lose touch with reality
And struggle to see how I fit in with those around me
So want I to share with my inner child and others made of such a mould
Is what you must find within yourself and cannot expect to be told
To better cope with the chorus of silence that neglect echoes.

Now I can't speak to you plainly
That wouldn't do much good
You weren't lucky enough to have mentors, role models and advisors
So a random such as I will not do.
But perhaps if I speak in verse
Your defences will give way
Like a coded message viewed from a mirror
Once read in reverse it will sound ok
Three poems are all I want to share
It's up to you if it's worth your time
Or a rude interruption into the silence you hear

❖❖❖

First Poem: No Recognition

There will be no recognition when you achieve wonderful things
No music, fanfare or medals given

Indeed, whether your talents lie in the arts, business or
simply being a decent person
No one will say "great job" in way that is satisfactory to you!
Your fruits will be plucked with no mind paid to the flower…
But that's fine, that's completely ok.
Flowers exists to be picked, pressed and fondled
They can handle affection without restraint
If they can, so can you!
With your many gifts you don't need any recognition
From others to know that such gifts exist.
So continue being beautiful, continue being true
Celebrate your own existence
Revel in the soil of your soul.

♦♦♦

Second Poem: No Fall from Grace

What can sometimes be worse, as strange as it is to say
Is not when without praise
But when others ignore your fall from grace
Yes, whilst you live your life as best you can
You will have moments when you're self-centred, selfish,
cruel and unkind
Nevertheless, you won't receive the judgment you deserve
Either too much blame or undue forgiveness
will not provide the healing that you yearn!
But don't fret or worry about the fairness of your lot
You are strong enough to own your fuck ups
You're not perfect and your judgment isn't fool proof
But you can learn from the bad that you do
Mistakes will teach lessons and make a better you.

♦♦♦

TREATMENT

Third Poem: No Redemption

Lesson learned, well done, great job!
That thing you did to hurt those you love?
Is no longer a problem since it is something you have overcome!
Yet as you return to Pride Rock to retake your throne
Animals won't be celebrating your return home
The Prodigal Son had a banquet
You'll have leftovers, long since turned cold
Yes, I know it sounds like it sucks
I know it's not the reception that the stories said would come
But sometimes the stories are wrong
What story said that you would come?
Yet here you are,
Yet here you are still!
Stories will be shared about the things you have achieved
Whether oral histories, idle chatter, songs or poems
But not today and maybe never during your days, dreams, after all, are for sleep.

♦♦♦

These three poems I have shared come from the heart
So, I hope that rings clearly whether you agree with me or not
That without encouragement you must learn to celebrate yourself
To praise yourself, blame yourself and appraise yourself.
I pray that it strengthens your legs and doesn't harden your heart.

Stop expecting to receive either love or hate.
Stop fearing failure and stop trying to escape
Instead learn to celebrate

Yes celebrate.
Then when you are fortunate enough to meet people you relate
to, ears used to silence will quiver without distraint.
Ready as you will be to participate.

TREATMENT

Me

Take my life and run with it
Take it wherever you want
Toss it around like a plaything
Love it as though it was yours
I give it to you packaged and clean
Full of all its problems, full of all its gifts
In this neat package I give you all of me
Just promise you will run with it
And take it somewhere free.

STAGE V

Ongoing Medication, or, Drugs

Where I provide a random assortment of poems that didn't fit elsewhere, whether that is due to their style or message, to bring this experience to a close.

TREATMENT

A Lesson

You broke your arm.
What, I broke your arm?
You are confused,
You broke your arm.
Remember?
You were climbing that tree in the yard;
one branch, then two, then three
Before gravity climbed you
and your arm tried to climb
out and away from your body.

You may have forgotten
Since it was quite the fall
But not only did you break your arm
You broke the tree as well!
To discourage other fools
from making similar mistakes
The branches were also removed
to prevent future aches.

Look outside your window,
Don't move too sharply lest you feel the pain.
That tree now stands as an obelisk
A testament to your failed traipse
Remember and never forget
as the tree regrows its branches
They will be clipped and cut as your arm
unfairly re-grows and becomes strong.
It is not my fault you sought to climb above
Your broken arm will heal but that tree will not.

Cry Blood

These moments of incidental poetry
Occur in every fight
Moments such as the one I am so
awed by, I take to keys and type:
"I saw Chudinov cry blood."

In a fight of little magnitude
A man's eyes kindly popped
to feed dry mouth
As Eubanks Jnr pummelled away
Swinging from left to right
A stubborn Russian was swayed
but somehow remained upright!
And with the expected win
The future looks very bright
For the man of famous lineage
Who won many fans last night
But as the crowd peels away
And the ring is embalmed in a
fetid dark
An ecstatic thought remains
"I saw Chudinov cry blood."

TREATMENT

Just Another Commute

The workers mill around a train station
as the train rattles past.
It makes the sound of a steam powered shuttle
Heading not to space but underground
Yet on this mundane day where all is as expected
Another rattle sends shudders through the earth
In the distance a beast built of metal scraps
Marches towards the train tracks.
Rising like the bastard child of London's industrial past
It is so much larger than the buildings it shatters and shreds.

Despite the summer heat snow falls from the sky
Although this snow is not cold, it still cuts as
it's blown across noses, cheeks and eyes.
It is the flecks of glass from buildings broken down
As the Giant marches through London.
Yet despite its noise and girth the workers do not stir
Oblivious as they are with sunken, sullen eyes
Already pale and weak from far too little sleep
They barely notice the Giant as they cannot distinguish
It from their collective nightmare of missing work
Granted mythical import by their phantasmal daydreaming.

Good Health

The problem with doctors
is that their product is sickness
They are desperate for the injured
Lest their careers be extinguished
But they needn't fear for as candlelight will stop,
and darkness will encroach where light is not,
So too is good health fleeting and far from the norm.

Doctors are not one's to seek advice
On how to live with the kinds of virtues
That could lead to their demise.

TREATMENT

00:31:24 AM

To capture a second and
turn into legible text
Is like nabbing a fly between chopsticks
Although not as hard as killing said fly
with said chopsticks
And not as hard as removing the smear
and grime of said fly's squashed torso
And not as hard as finding new chopsticks
To catch and kill said flies' kin
Still humming at 00:31:24 AM.

Journeymen

What drives?
    Like steel through stake
        Through hand, wood and bone
A sacrificial lamb
Willingly into the slaughterhouse
Knowing they might not return?

Men and women with kneaded bodies,
padded hands and jeering fans
Toughened skin and broken nose
Swollen eyes and vaseline soaked cheekbones
Where defeat is expected and a beating accepted.

They are Journeymen:
Scraggy lambs,
overweight,
undersized,
"Tomato cans"
The mould of fistic gold.

TREATMENT

Speak no Evil

Cut the cruelty from the tongue
Because such a pretty shade of red
Should be saved for rosé and not used to offend.

Cut the venom, cut the glands
That spit and scatter acidic threads
Until the fat is cast aside and all that
is left is pure, smooth and kind.

A tongue, such a muscle, such a slab
Ought to leak clear fluids and not litres
putrid, coagulated and bad.

Obedient, Given Time

"10080 minutes" spoke the clock
As the nought shifted up from a nine
He did as he was instructed
Walked a lap around the room
Drank water, had food
Before sitting down and pretending to answer calls.

"10080 minutes" the clock spoke once more
He had lost count of how many weeks he'd spent alone,
nevertheless he continued to work as payment was due.
This experiment had made him grim
but promised great wealth once he had seen it through.
Is a man capable of dreams if he is denied sleep?
Can a dreamless man have a future without
sleep to separate the present from the past
and days from weeks?

"10080 minutes" the clock would say for the final time
The man was chipper as he worked his 9 to 5
According to the camera he was still alone
However he spoke aloud as though other people
filled the room.
He no longer pretended to answer the phone
Driven mad he heard the ring and spoke to a friend
invented entirely by him!

TREATMENT

The Greatest of All Times

Come if you have courage
If you have the intelligence, wit and might
The dedication to face hours of monotonous pain
Calloused knuckles, bent nose, shattered eye sockets
Eye sockets starved of eyes.

They call him the G.O.A.T:
The Greatest of All Times
There will be no republic
as he is dictator for life
No not life but all lives
His reign is endless as before him
there was no greatest
Only great and greater indeed there was
no test such as that faced by his challengers.

Come if you have courage
If you have ignorance and self-directed spite
For even in victory you can never be:
The Greatest of All Times.

Miles Raphael

The Other Choice

So here we are, what have we found
As on knees you feel the gun between your teeth
Voice says "Give me what I want or gun will speak"
Soul steps out of brain and out of body.

Is this the final flash before you die?
Will you now relive every second of your life?
Has the bullet already blown through your brain?
Is that why you're talking to me as though insane?
We all have that voice inside our heads
Belonging to no one we have met
It speaks and tries to show us something else
That for every right turn a left could have been taken as well.

Printed in Poland
by Amazon Fulfillment
Poland Sp. z o.o., Wrocław